THE MLB FAN'S GUIDE

12 REASONS TO LOVE THE ATLANTA BRAVES

by Jonathan Kronstadt

12 STORY LIBRARY

www.12StoryLibrary.com

12-Story Library is an imprint of Peterson Publishing Company and Press Room Editions.

Produced for 12-Story Library by Red Line Editorial

Photographs ©: John Bazemore/AP Images, cover, 1, 5, 11, 28; Pat Sullivan/AP Images, 6; Tom DiPace/AP Images, 7; AP Images, 9, 12, 13, 15, 23; Charles Kelly/AP Images, 17; Jim Mone/AP Images, 18, 29; Hans Deryk/AP Images, 20; Mark Duncan/AP Images, 21; Erik S. Lesser/AP Images, 25; Dave Martin/AP Images, 27

ISBN
978-1-63235-207-1 (hardcover)
978-1-63235-234-7 (paperback)
978-1-62143-259-3 (hosted ebook)

Library of Congress Control Number: 2015934312

Printed in the United States of America
Mankato, MN
October, 2015

TABLE OF CONTENTS

1

BRAVES WIN 14 STRAIGHT DIVISION TITLES

It began on October 5, 1991. The Atlanta Braves beat the Houston Astros for their eighth win in a row. With it, they clinched the National League (NL) West division title. It began an amazing streak of 14 straight division titles.

The streak actually ran until 2005. That's because a players' strike ended the 1994 season early. No team won division titles that year. Only the New York Yankees can come close to the Braves' record winning streak. New York reached the playoffs 13 consecutive seasons from 1995 to 2007.

5

NL pennants won by the Braves from 1991 to 2005.

- Atlanta beat the Cleveland Indians to win their only World Series in 1995.
- The Braves won at least 100 games six times, including a team-record 106 in 1998.
- They spent 1,632 days in first place during their 14-year run.

THINK ABOUT IT

Despite the Braves' success, they won only a single World Series. The Yankees won four over the same 15-year period. Do you still consider the Braves to be a great success? Or does a team have to win championships to be successful? Use examples to make your point.

Every summer in Atlanta was a winner. The Braves won 60.6 percent of their games from 1991 to 2005. That is an average of 98 wins per year.

Dozens of players had a role in the streak. Atlanta always had a strong pitching staff. "The Big Three" pitchers of Tom Glavine, Greg Maddux, and John Smoltz led the way. Smoltz later became the team's dominant closer.

Atlanta had no shortage of bats, though. Great hitters such as Chipper Jones, Andruw Jones, and Gary Sheffield played major roles, too. And the people running the team—president Stan Kasten, general manager John Schuerholz, and field manager Bobby Cox—were there the whole time.

Andruw Jones (left) and Rafael Furcal celebrate the Braves' 2005 division title.

2

"THE BIG THREE" ARE MASTERS OF THE MOUND

Tom Glavine first pitched for the Atlanta Braves in 1987. John Smoltz pitched his first game one year later. Then Greg Maddux joined the team in 1993. The trio became known as "The Big Three." They played together in Atlanta until 2002. Few pitching trios could compare.

John Smoltz pitches in a 1998 game.

The Big Three combined to win 648 games for the Braves. And they did it in very different ways.

Maddux was nicknamed "The Professor." He didn't overpower hitters. Instead he tricked them with the movement on his pitches. Glavine had excellent control. He could throw fast or slow—and always on target. Smoltz had the best fastball of the bunch. He also had a quick-diving split-finger pitch.

Each member of the Big Three won a Cy Young Award while with the Braves. All three are in the Baseball Hall of Fame, too. They also led the Braves in the team's most successful era. In the 10 years they were teammates, the trio led the Braves to the playoffs nine times. The only time they missed the playoffs was in 1994. But no team made the playoffs that year. The season never finished due to a players' strike. But the Braves came back in 1995 and won their only World Series since they moved to Atlanta in 1966.

Tom Glavine (left) and Greg Maddux in 1994

17

Combined All-Star Game selections for the Braves' Big Three.

- They combined to win six NL Cy Young Awards as Braves.
- Greg Maddux led the NL in earned-run average (ERA) four times.
- Tom Glavine was the 1995 World Series Most Valuable Player (MVP).
- John Smoltz is the only pitcher with at least 200 wins and 150 saves.

SPAHN AND SAIN AND PRAY FOR RAIN

The Braves still played in Boston in 1948. Warren Spahn and Johnny Sain were their best pitchers. The pitchers were so good that a local sports editor wrote a poem about them. In the poem he hoped for two days of rain after the two stars pitched. That way they'd be rested and able to pitch every game. The team's slogan became "Spahn and Sain and Pray for Rain."

3

BRAVES ARE ON THE MOVE

The Braves have played in Atlanta since 1966. But the team is much older than that. In fact, the Braves are the oldest team in Major League Baseball (MLB).

They started as the Boston Red Stockings in 1871. The Red Stockings won four National Association championships. Then they moved to the brand new NL in 1876.

In 1883, the Red Stockings changed their name to the Beaneaters. The new name kept the team from being confused with another team called the Reds. The name changed twice more over the years. Then in 1912, the name was changed again. This time it became the Braves. The team won the World Series in 1914. But the Braves didn't play in the World Series again until 1948. Attendance fell over the next few years. The crosstown Red Sox proved to be more popular. So the Braves moved to Milwaukee in 1953.

The Braves were an instant hit in Milwaukee. They set a league attendance record their first year there. They won the World Series

1.8 million

Fans who came to see the Braves play their first year in Milwaukee.

- The legendary Babe Ruth ended his career with the Boston Braves in 1935, but the team lost 115 games.
- The Braves are older than the World Series. It began in 1903.
- No major US professional sports team has been around as long as the Braves.

The Milwaukee Braves' Eddie Mathews hits his 400th career home run in 1963.

in 1957. But the team was sold in 1962. The new owners quickly started looking for a new home. They found one in the growing city of Atlanta. The city built a brand new stadium for the team. So the Braves moved there in 1966. The Atlanta area has been their home ever since.

EDDIE MATHEWS MAKES THE MOVE

Eddie Mathews joined the Boston Braves in 1952. He moved with the Braves to Milwaukee in 1953. Then he came along to Atlanta when the Braves moved there in 1966. Mathews was the only Braves player to play in all three cities. The hall of fame third baseman hit 493 home runs in his 15 seasons with the Braves. Mathews spent his final two seasons with other teams.

4

CHIPPER JONES IS FIRST AT THIRD

The Braves had the first pick in the 1990 MLB Draft. They wanted to pick pitcher Todd Van Poppel. But he said he wouldn't sign with them. So instead they picked Chipper Jones. It turned out to be the better pick. Van Poppel had a solid career as a journeyman. Jones became one of the greatest third basemen in baseball history.

Jones made his debut with the Braves late in the 1993 season. However, he hurt his knee and didn't play in 1994. The following year he helped the Braves win the World Series. That year also marked the first of 11 straight years the team made the playoffs with Jones.

Jones led the team with his strong hitting. He could hit for average or for power. And as a switch-hitter, he was a threat from both sides of the plate. In 1999, Jones hit .319 with 45 homers and 110 runs batted in (RBIs). He was named NL MVP.

Jones announced he would retire after the 2012 season. It was his 19th season. All were with the Braves. Opposing teams honored Jones when the Braves visited each city for the last time. They had good reason. He finished his career with 1,623 RBIs. That was more than any other third baseman in history. The Braves honored him in another way. They retired his No. 10 jersey.

0

Switch-hitters besides Chipper Jones who hit .300 and had more than 400 home runs in their careers.

- Jones was named to eight All-Star Games.
- He was the NL batting champion in 2008, when he batted .364.

Chipper Jones hits his 400th career home run in 2008.

5

BRAVES BRING 1957 TITLE TO MILWAUKEE

The first World Series was held in 1903. The Boston Braves went twice, winning once. In 1957, the Milwaukee Braves won their first NL pennant. Winning the World Series would be a spectacular task, though. The American League-champion New York Yankees had won six of the past eight World Series. The Braves were ready, though. Slugger Hank Aaron and pitcher Warren Spahn led the way.

The World Series turned in Milwaukee's favor on a dab of shoe polish. New York won two of the first three games. In Game 4, the Braves blew a three-run lead in the ninth inning. Then the Yankees went ahead in the top of the 10th inning.

Pinch hitter Nippy Jones led off for the Braves in the bottom of the 10th. One of the pitches went right toward Jones's shoe. Jones claimed it hit him. The umpire disagreed. Then Jones pointed out a spot of

The Braves' Wes Covington makes a back-handed catch in the 1957 World Series.

Lew Burdette pitches in Game 7 of the 1957 World Series.

shoe polish on the ball. With that, the umpire sent him to first base.

Two batters later, shortstop Johnny Logan drove in the game-tying run. Then third baseman Eddie Mathews homered to win it 7–5.

Braves pitcher Lew Burdette shut the Yankees out in Games 5 and 7. That gave the city of Milwaukee its first World Series championship.

SPITBALL?

Some people accused Lew Burdette of throwing an illegal spitball. Burdette never admitted to throwing a spitball. But he seemed to want people to think he did. "Let them think I throw it," he said. "That gives me an edge, because it is another pitch they have to worry about."

0.67

Lew Burdette's ERA in the 1957 World Series.

- Burdette won three games in the Series and was MVP.
- Burdette started Game 7 on just two days of rest because scheduled starter Warren Spahn had the flu.
- Hank Aaron batted .393 in the Series.
- In 1958, Burdette was the losing pitcher in Game 7 of the World Series rematch against the Yankees.

6

ANDY MESSERSMITH IS BASEBALL'S FIRST FREE AGENT

For many years, baseball players were tied to one team. The player contracts had something called the "reserve clause." It gave teams the right to keep players year after year. Players could only switch teams if they were traded or released. Andy Messersmith changed that.

Messersmith was a star pitcher with the Los Angeles Dodgers in 1975. The team wanted to re-sign him using the reserve clause. But it had done so the previous season, too. So Messersmith argued he was now a free agent. He filed a grievance with the players' union. The case went to an arbitrator, who's sort of like a judge. The arbitrator said Messersmith could sign with any team he wanted. So he signed with the Braves.

This case changed baseball forever. Now after a certain number of

THINK ABOUT IT

Andy Messersmith was baseball's first free agent. How has free agency improved the game for players and teams? Have there been any negatives from free agency? If so, what are they?

$1 million

Amount the Braves paid Andy Messersmith over his three-year contract.

- Messersmith allowed just 6.9 hits per nine innings in his career.
- That was the sixth lowest total ever.

years in the major leagues, players become free agents. They can sign with any team that wants them. Teams now have to bid for the best players. Salaries have skyrocketed. Messersmith wasn't as successful with the Braves as he had been earlier in his career. But his decision to fight for his rights ended up improving the lives of the players that came after him.

The Braves' Andy Messersmith pitches in a 1976 game.

7

TBS SUPERSTATION SENDS BRAVES COAST TO COAST

Cable TV was little more than an idea in the early 1970s. Americans only had a few broadcast channels. Local baseball games were shown on TV. But fans weren't able to watch many out-of-town games. The Braves changed that.

It all started when Ted Turner bought the Braves in 1976. Turner had made millions in his billboard business. He already owned a local TV station, too. With cable TV growing, Turner got on board. In 1977, he sent Braves' broadcasts by satellite from WTBS to cable television stations all over the country. Soon the Braves were winning fans from coast to coast. Turner called WTBS a "superstation." Because the Braves were shown around the country, he nicknamed them "America's Team."

The Braves weren't very good in the early days of WTBS, which later became known as TBS. But pretty soon they were winning games to go along with all the fans they'd won. In 1997, they moved to a new stadium named Turner Field. And guess who threw out the first pitch at the first game? Yep, Ted Turner.

32

Years in which Braves games were broadcast on WTBS, ending in 2007.

- Ted Turner bought the Braves in part as programming for his WTBS superstation.
- Turner used SATCOM 1, an early communications satellite, to beam Braves games coast-to-coast.

Team owner Ted Turner cheers on the Braves during a 1982 game.

WACKY PROMOTIONS

Ted Turner also tried to make going to Braves games more fun. He held a frog-jumping contest and encouraged fans to bring their own frogs. He put on a Braves Olympics. Turner won an event called The Great Baseball Nose Push. He had to get down on all fours and push a baseball around the bases with his nose.

8

BRAVES GO FROM WORST TO FIRST

Braves fans didn't have much to cheer for in the late 1980s. The team lost 106 games in 1988. That began a three-year streak of last-place finishes. They won just 65 games in 1990. The division-champion Cincinnati Reds won 91. No one expected the Braves to come within one run of winning the 1991 World Series. But that's exactly what they did. The first World Series was in 1903. Until 1991, no team had gone from worst to first.

The Braves' Mark Lemke scores a run in the 1991 World Series.

29

Games the Braves improved in 1991 over 1990.

- The Braves gave up 177 fewer runs in 1991.
- The Braves and Pittsburgh Pirates played three 1-0 games in the NLCS. That was a record for a postseason series.

WHAT ARE THE ODDS?

The American Association's Louisville Colonels went from worst to first in 1890. No major league team did it again until 1991. And that year, both the Braves and Minnesota Twins did it. Those teams met in a wild World Series that year. Minnesota won when pitcher Jack Morris threw 10 scoreless innings in Game 7.

The Braves' improvement began with some new players who turned out to be key players. First baseman Sid Bream provided a veteran presence. Outfielder Otis Nixon was second in the NL with 72 stolen bases. The Braves also added third baseman Terry Pendleton. He had never played in an All-Star Game. Then he won the NL MVP Award in his first year in Atlanta.

Meanwhile, young Braves players improved. Outfielders David Justice and Ron Gant provided home run power. Three young starting pitchers played a key role, too. Steve Avery Tom Glavine, and John Smoltz combined to win 27 games in 1990. They won 52 in 1991.

The fans responded. Attendance at Atlanta-Fulton County Stadium doubled. More than 2 million fans attended games in 1991.

The Braves held off the Pittsburgh Pirates in an exciting, seven-game NL Championship Series (NLCS). The World Series against the Minnesota Twins went seven games, too. But the Braves fell 1–0 in the final game. Some consider it to be the best World Series Game 7 of all time.

9

BRAVES WIN WORLD SERIES—FINALLY!

Cleveland Indians batter Carlos Baerga launched a deep fly ball. Braves center fielder Marquis Grissom got underneath it. He squeezed the ball in his glove. With that out, the Braves had won the 1995 World Series. As the team celebrated, a Braves fan held up a sign. It simply read: "Finally."

The Braves had been one of baseball's best teams in the 1990s. They reached the 1991 and 1992 World Series. Then they got to the 1993 NLCS. But fans were still waiting for the team's first championship. The Braves' last title had come in 1957. They still played in Milwaukee then.

The 1995 Braves were loaded. All-Star first baseman Fred McGriff had 27 home runs and 93 RBIs. Young third baseman Chipper Jones added 86 RBIs. And catcher

The Braves' Fred McGriff blasts a home run in Game 1 of the 1995 World Series.

Braves pitcher Mark Wohlers lifts catcher Javy Lopez in celebration after winning the 1995 World Series.

Javy Lopez led the team with a .315 batting average. Meanwhile, the Braves' pitching was typically dominant. Greg Maddux won his fourth straight NL Cy Young Award. Tom Glavine was third in Cy Young voting.

Atlanta ran away with the NL East with a 90–54 record. Then the Braves beat the Colorado Rockies and swept the Cincinnati Reds in the NL playoffs. That set up the World Series against Cleveland.

The Braves won the first two games. Cleveland came back and won two of the next three games. But Game 6 was Atlanta's. Glavine gave up just one hit in eight innings. David Justice hit a home run. Then closer Mark Wohlers finished the 1–0 shutout in the ninth. The Braves had won the World Series. Finally!

5

Games decided by one run in the six-game 1995 World Series.

- Cleveland hadn't been in the World Series since 1954.
- Cleveland averaged almost six runs per game in the regular season but just three in the World Series.

10

HANK AARON BECOMES BASEBALL'S HOME RUN KING

Hank Aaron hit his first major league home run on April 23, 1954. He was a 20-year-old rookie with the Milwaukee Braves. Almost 20 years later, he hit home run 715. That broke Babe Ruth's career home run record. Aaron ended with 755 home runs. He hit all but 22 wearing a Braves uniform.

Aaron began his professional career in the Negro Leagues. For years, MLB teams refused to sign black players like Aaron. That finally changed in the 1940s. Aaron debuted with the Braves in 1954. He proved to be excellent at hitting, throwing, fielding, and running. But he became famous for hitting home runs. He led the league in home runs four times. He had 15 seasons with at least 30 homers.

Aaron ended the 1973 season with 713 home runs. That was one shy of Ruth's record. Many fans didn't want Aaron to break the record. Ruth was a beloved player in baseball history. Some racist fans hated the idea of a black man breaking Ruth's record. Many of these fans sent Aaron hate mail. They threatened him. But Aaron got letters of support, too.

Aaron tied Ruth's record on his first swing of the 1974 season. Four days later he broke the record before 53,775 cheering fans at Atlanta-Fulton County Stadium.

BATTING BROTHERS

Hank Aaron and younger brother Tommie both played for the Braves. Tommie hit only 13 home runs in seven seasons. But together the brothers hit 768 homers. That is a record for brothers.

2,297

RBIs by Hank Aaron over his career, an MLB record.

- Barry Bonds broke Aaron's career home run record in 2007 and ended with 762.
- Bonds has been linked with illegal performance-enhancing drugs, tarnishing the record.

Hank Aaron hits his record 715th home run.

11

THE BRAVES BATTLE BEHIND BOBBY COX

Hundreds of players wore an Atlanta Braves uniform from 1991 to 2010. But they had only one manager: Bobby Cox.

Cox had not been a great baseball player. But he proved to be one of baseball's best managers. He first managed the Braves from 1978 to 1981. Then the team fired Cox. The Braves front office wanted better results. Cox got better results with the Toronto Blue Jays. His teams had three winning seasons in four years. After the 1985 season, the Braves brought Cox back as general manager. He took on manager duties again during the 1990 season. One year later the team began its streak of 14 consecutive division titles.

Cox was known for his calm approach with players. "I always said he had more patience than grandma," said third baseman Terry Pendleton. Cox always made a point to stand up for his players. When a player started arguing with an

16

Seasons in which Bobby Cox's teams made the playoffs.

- All but one of those seasons was with the Braves.
- Cox led the Toronto Blue Jays to within one game of the 1985 World Series.

THINK ABOUT IT

How do you think Bobby Cox's ejections affected his team? Do you think it helped players, knowing the manager had their backs? Or do you think it hurt the team to lose the manager for the rest of the game?

umpire, Cox stepped in. This led to him being ejected 158 times. That is an MLB record. But by being ejected, Cox often saved his player from being kicked out of the game instead.

Cox retired in 2010. He won 2,504 games as a manager. That was the fourth highest total ever. He was inducted into the Baseball Hall of Fame in 2014.

An umpire ejects Bobby Cox from a 2000 game.

12

TURNER FIELD IS A BALLPARK OF OLYMPIC PROPORTIONS

The Braves moved into Atlanta-Fulton County Stadium in 1966. There were few highlights. The team lost more games than it won. Attendance was often low. And the Braves had to share the stadium with the Atlanta Falcons football team. By the early 1990s, the Braves were looking to move to a new home.

They got their wish. The 1996 Olympics were in Atlanta. Olympic organizers gave their stadium to the Braves when the Games ended. The team made many changes. It ripped out the running track and approximately 35,000 seats. A new Grand Entry Plaza was built. When construction wrapped up, the Braves had themselves a proper ballpark.

WHAT A YEAR

On August 1, 1996, a crowd of 82,884 fans packed into Centennial Olympic Stadium in Atlanta. They were there to witness history. Michael Johnson delivered. Wearing gold shoes, the US sprinter raced to his second gold medal of the 1996 Olympics. And in this race, the 200-meter dash, he set a world record. Nearly five months later, on April 4, 1997, a crowd of 45,044 fans showed up to the same stadium. History was made again as the Braves played their first game in Turner Field. They came back in the eighth inning to beat the Chicago Cubs 5–4 in the stadium opener.

Fans cheer on the Braves at Turner Field during the 2013 playoffs.

Turner Field opened at the start of the 1997 season.

The view of downtown Atlanta to the north was an attraction. So was the view on the field. The Braves won division titles in their first nine seasons at Turner Field. In 1999, they made the World Series.

Turner Field proved to be a memorable home for the Braves. But it wasn't a long-term home. The Braves planned a new ballpark to open for the 2017 season. It's located 10 miles (16.1 km) north of Atlanta in Cobb County.

71 x 79

Feet, in height and width (21.6 x 24.1 m), of the video board installed at Turner Field in 2005. That made it the biggest outdoor high-definition video screen in the world at the time.

- Turner Field was built next to Atlanta-Fulton County Stadium.
- Atlanta-Fulton County Stadium was demolished after the 1996 Olympics.

12 KEY DATES

1871
The Braves' franchise starts out as the Boston Red Stockings.

1876
The Red Stockings win the first NL game ever, beating the Philadelphia Athletics 6–5.

1912
The team—which had been known as the Red Stockings, Beaneaters, Doves, and Rustlers—changes its name to the Braves.

1914
The Miracle Braves, who started out the season 4–18, come from last place on July 18 to win the NL pennant and sweep the Philadelphia A's in the World Series.

1953
The Braves play their first season in Milwaukee before an NL-record 1.8 million fans at brand-new Milwaukee County Stadium.

1957
The Braves win the World Series over the New York Yankees. Slugger Hank Aaron and pitcher Lew Burdette lead the way.

1966
The Braves move to Atlanta and brand-new Atlanta-Fulton County Stadium.

1976
Ted Turner buys the Braves and starting in 1977 broadcasts their games around the country on his cable channel, WTBS.

1991
The Braves go from last place one season to first place the next, but lose in the World Series to the Minnesota Twins—who also went worst to first that season.

1995
Led by a terrific pitching staff, the Braves win their first World Series since moving to Atlanta. Tom Glavine pitches eight shutout innings in Game 6 to clinch the title.

1997
The Braves move into newly constructed Turner Field. It had been the main stadium during the 1996 Olympics.

2010
Longtime Braves manager Bobby Cox retires. Under his leadership the team won the division every season it was awarded from 1991 to 2005 and won the 1995 World Series.

GLOSSARY

contract
A legal agreement between two parties, such as a baseball player and a team. A baseball contract determines things like salary and years of service.

draft
A system leagues use to spread incoming talent among all the teams. The teams pick players in order of how they finished the previous season, with the worst team picking first.

eject
To kick someone out of a game as punishment.

free agent
A player who is not signed by a team and is allowed to sign with any team.

general manager
The person in charge of putting together a baseball team's roster and coaching staff.

grievance
A complaint.

pennant
A league championship.

rookie
A first-year player in a league.

satellite
A machine that is sent into space and orbits a planet.

strike
When workers refuse to work in protest of conditions.

union
A group of workers who come together to try to achieve common goals.

FOR MORE INFORMATION

Books

Christopher, Matt. *On The Mound With . . . Greg Maddux.* New York: Hachette, 2009.

Jacobs, Greg, and Joe Gergen. *The Everything Kids' Baseball Book, 8th Edition.* Avon, MA: Adams Media, 2014.

Stewart, Mark. *The Atlanta Braves.* Chicago: Norwood House, 2012.

Websites

Atlanta Braves

atlanta.braves.mlb.com

Baseball Reference

www.baseball-reference.com

Major League Baseball

www.mlb.com

INDEX

About the Author

Jonathan Kronstadt has written books for children on everything from sports to dinosaurs to deep-sea creatures. He has also written scripts for many museum exhibits and videos. He lives in Silver Spring, Maryland.